Antidotes for Life

— RICHARD GREEN —

An every-day man's book of awareness, a sideways ramble through living today and how to stay on top of it; a philosophy for Life, the Universe and Everything Else… possibly… and featuring a Little Book of 'R' Words.

An environmentally friendly book printed and bound in England by
www.printondemand-worldwide.com

This book is made entirely of chain-of-custody materials

www.fast-print.net/store.php

Antidotes for Life
Copyright © Richard Green 2012

All rights reserved

No part of this book may be reproduced in any form by photocopying or any electronic or mechanical means, including information storage or retrieval systems, without permission in writing from both the copyright owner and the publisher of the book.

ISBN 978-178035-450-7

First published 2012 by
FASTPRINT PUBLISHING
Peterborough, England.
Printed by Printondemand-Worldwide

- At Work
- Sex
- Love
- People
- Food
- Money
- Fearweather Friends (poem)
- Success

Resistance
Results
Religion –
- Personal God
- Churches
- On Sundays (poem)

Reasoning -
- Questions
- Answers
- Change is Constant

Artists
Safety Valve
Nuggets
Everything is Cool (poem)
Responsibility
The 'F' Word
King Clown (poem)
Remembrances
Spooky Stuff (Quantum)
Spooky Stuff (Tao)
On Enlightenment
The Theory of Everything #1 (poem)

The Theory of Everything #2
On Spirituality
Healing Practice
Healing #1 (poem)
Healing #2 (poem)
Healing Prayer
Misc. Poems –
- I Weep for Generations
- On Society
- To the Unknown Lover
- Awaiting
- Our Homes

Jottings From My Blotting Papers
Musings
And Finally
Suggested Further Reading
End Page
Acknowledgements
About the Author

On Writing.

Pens move over a surface
Trailing words
From poets, peasants and sage.
Moving on in letters or books
The reader to engage;
Leading him and her
To a new understanding.

Why 'Antidote for Life'?

For many, Life is about being pushed about from pillar to post by bosses, spouses, children, tv, the internet, the 'system', society in general. All making demands on your time, of which there's never enough for living your dreams; supposing you do dream

So, how to deal with this and get some balance into your own life, the one really yearned for, to live and flow with?

Well, maybe this will help….

If you're not happy with any or some of what you read in the following missive; refer to the End Page for guidance.

Introduction

You say to me (the author) :

"What's the purpose of yet another 'personal development' whatsit book; I've got dozens on my bookshelves already, none have changed my life like the jacket-cover said it would?"

Right.

Good question

Promise - This book you're holding now may help move your life on, but it's up to you to commit to an idea expressed. that you can go with; Live it, hear it, drink it, smell it, taste it, touch it, love it, see it. Above all see it. Understand what's being said and feel it within you. Only then will it make any sense, only then can you deal with it and make any progress, in your own way and in your own time.

This book is a pointer, another way of looking at things, challenging you to challenge (viz: look at again), your values .A stepping stone to...? And I, the author, make no claim to accuracy of any 'facts', all mistakes (if so) are gloriously mine, but hopefully they will also illustrate or demonstrate a point and get you thinking...

We are not perfect, except in our imperfections; being perfect is more than anyone can bear or needs. Neither are we, (the book or the author) setting out to start a new 'Movement to Change' anything. It's just about now and then and dealing with now and then, a touch non-p.c. in places it may be argued... see what it brings to you. Bless you my friend for you are on your path, whether you know it or not. Don't get caught up too much in this idea of seeking your Path; as I say, you are already on it; an idea that is expressed in the Buddhist tradition as: "If you can't find the truth right where you are, where else do you think you will find it?" This book needed be written... by me, apparently... so here it is. Namaste.

Speaking Out

Breaking faith with the Tao, for just now, in speaking out, having a say, going own way, getting outside those insidious boxes that are suffocating progress.

By obeying my instincts am being true to my true nature, while having nothing to prove, there's lots to lose by remaining quiet.

Problems with Life are usually in the status quo, going against the flow is an answer for you to decide. You may deride this book, but at least I've had a look facing the challenge to write the dam' thing.

Facing / embracing your issues helps them go away; encouraging to have your say, who knows from where knowledge flows, so discover that maybe Life is it's own antidote to life!, so put away the tissues.   And this it what it's all about...

On Politics

The realization our leaders (bless 'em) do not know, is, they'll not go where none has gone before; in the end they die political deaths, even in their last breaths don't see their limited scope.   Having to U-turn or resign against their grand design, politicking a contract in hope.   The difficulty is easy to identify; as Albert Einstein observed: "The problems of today cannot be solved with the same mind-set that created them in the first place".

So if you want change, be a force to rearrange the Rules for the wise and fools come the next election; suggest votes for that one who knows best how to get 'Order and Things Done'.   In this your very own hairdressers and taxi drivers are number one.   Lollipop ladies (and gents too), with no nonsense manifestos. Talk to them to change the rules governing N.H.S., fat cats and the schools.

The further from Westminster you are the less relevance it has; pretty poor state of affairs; so there you goes with all those cares, what can be done? Now you know!   Well it's a thought. What's needed is to get away from Party politics and political dogma, and a bit more thinking about stuff in a more non-pc and commonsense way, in terms of what will actually work and be of real use.

But of course there's a bit more to it than that...

On the Human Condition

We humans are complex beings, animals in a physical sense, but more than other animals as we have the ability to contemplate death, our own especially. All other life accepts death as just being part of the process and cycle of existence as in the seasons; birth and rebirth. We are conscious soul beings within a body for our journey on this planet called Earth. This soul also has Psyche and a free will, within which is Mind, (dealing with thought and consciousness), Ego, (the bit that works between conscious and un-conscious, our view of reality and identity).

Superego deals with conscience and survival instincts with our intelligence. Psyche is the place where evil comes from, evil being a relative term, and is made of primitive survival mixed in with a good dose of vanity.

When you review what Mankind has done and is still yet doing, it doesn't take long to realize there's no divine plan behind life. It's the work of the devil, except there is no devil. ' Ain't no devil but us'. (The Divine Plan for Life, however, is quite a different matter). By extension of this idea any person who wishes to rule the world is by definition then, quite the wrong guy (or gal) for the job, this because of the of the poor ego's desire for power and then being subject to the corrupting influences of that power and privilege.

It's not all gloom, look around at this beautiful place we live on, marvel at the good we're also a part of; there's plenty to wonder at.

Everything is all about balance and our awareness for balance, avoiding extremes like black and white; absence of colour against all the colours combined. Forget shades of grey, shadings of every hue more like it.

For every thought and idea there's a contrary one. e.g.- Richard Dawkins has written of The God Delusion – that's right! there's a book called The Science Delusion. Two books actually with that title I've found; one by Rupert Sheldrake and the other by Peter Wilberg, who writes…"why God is real and science is religious myth…"Ergo: You pays your money and takes your choice…

In nature we find 'triple balance', which shows that ultimately balance is possible...gas, liquid and solid coming together, with air and water, as ice.

For anything to exist there has to be an equal and opposite, a male to female, a balance; thus problems of any kind are much to do with imbalances. Incarnate here we are, spirit dragging around our physical frame...

We have spirit, which is reckoned to reside in the heart, as emotions and feelings – our true selves – in the head we find thought and ego for our potential balances.

The yin and yang coupling of the Taijitu symbol demonstrates this balancing concept very well, neither component is superior in any way; rather, their nature is a complementary one. The yin and yang (light and shade) curls contain a part of the other within itself, a diagrammatic clue that solutions are often contained in the problem?

Heart and soul is in a place of love.

Head and ego is in a place of uncertainty. When calm, detached, seeing with the eyes in your inner heart, it's accepted that events happen for a reason, though not always understood. The ego is prone to run around in confusion, afraid of what might happen next, or in fear of some loss, or even simple embarrassment.

Your heart can be heard in the quiet, the stillness, as in meditation, be moved by all of nature's beauty – sunsets, trees, mountains or waves upon the shore.

The ego speaks in unending chatter never allowing peace. This is what calls you away to play when better off at work; or indeed, the other way round, keeping you in self-defeating habits; the 'devil' in all scriptures.

Jesus was tempted after spending 40 days in the wilderness... with all His power and knowledge and purity, the monkey chatter said 'if you want you can rule the world and make slaves of all the peasants'.

Classic

Ego having a go; uncertain and afraid of Jesu's soul's life purpose and plan.

Everything we do is from belief, out of ego's drive of negativity in point of purpose, results and the vanities; or else from love, compassion, respect for our earthly home, other people (who've as much right to be here as you do), the plant and animal domains too.

From our hearts we do no harm.

From our ego and fears is greed, disregard for others in climbing social ladders or attaining more wealth than necessary... works of the 'devil' within; reality versus unreality,; positive energy versus negative, if you will...

If You Got It

If you got it, no need to flaunt it, because those that can, do. Those that can't, teach. A bit unfair that, there's some good teachers out there who can also do but wish to share their expertise and love of subject; not all those that can, can teach either, for teaching is a two-way process; a bit of give and take and rapport with their pupils, wouldn't you say?

Apparently those that can't teach, lecture – a one way process, like tv, Ah! This is what (self) appointed experts are about, with 'summat t' prove' or convince you of, who usually protest a bit too much leaving one wondering who it really is they're needing to convince… ? Ho hum.

Dear Thought

A dear thought has to me been shown
And if not noted this instant
Will be gone, non returning, lost
Into the distant unknown,
And at a cost to our learning.
Dear thought, have we met before
In another circumstance?
Or glimpsed in a dream by chance
Beyond the limitation and frontier
That's accepted as only too real,
In the romance of worldly fear?
If not writ large will be drown'd
In the whole.
Only hope that someday
Dear thought you
May be found...
By a more diligent soul.

On Perceptions

If you ponder on life and lives all that much, you'll probably realize most people are sheep, following one of two kinds of shepherd – the good 'uns or those who abuse the authority and power given them. Power given; because that is it's nature, power is only released (given away) by what you believe.

If in a position of authority – with or without the capital A – most likely you'll be abusing that privilege somehow. viz: taking advantage. Giving in to corrupting influences is in the nature of power... along with it's being an aphrodisiac for some.

In these pages there's stuff already known to you, except may have to have read it here to realize you already knew it! That's often the way it works, this knowledge thing. Perceptions are what our brains decode from physical senses' information about the reality of this whole Shebang; made of atoms colliding in an almost empty expanding space, making it seem solid. Quantum theory demonstrates life is an illusion; and if that's not enough already, memory creates further illusions, as in linear time, for example.

It's said there's nothing new under the Sun; but of course there is, just look around the world, nature re-creating through the seasons, for example it's also widely believed that no two snowflakes are ever the same... just think about *that* for a minute or two...

If an idea in this book gets your attention there's a list at the back for some suggested further reading... see where it takes you and find new answers continually adding to this, experience. What you know and believe is largely to be found in that toolbox. Don't take anyone's word before testing to own satisfaction; be prepared though to modify the new view even next day in light of newer information; there's no absolutes!

To know what you know because you know it is true is empowering... and why you're not a sheep.

Be careful what you take on trust, intuition tells about this; if you have to be asked to trust... is that because they don't trust themselves? Governments and Churches since forever are the worst offenders in this. The purpose of these institutions is to maintain their position and hide the truth. Read your history books, against mankind the gods themselves have contended in vain; all part of the human condition, created by ourselves – to lie about even the smallest things; plus thinking that wars are o.k.

Nobody has a monopoly on the truth, though plenty folk will tell you they do; you may know a few of 'em... I bet they're always right and equally unhappy. Well, with all that guilt and judgement, it's enough to weigh anyone down.

Through the unlocked doors in your mind, which you may have thought locked to you, are all possibilities. Asking questions of life in the light of new experiences, be prepared to change beliefs again! and still be comfortable with yourself – in fact be even more comfortable *within* yourself. Give yourself permission, in having no claim, other than to *be,* for why shouldn't you be the referee in your own game; always remembering no-one is on the Ref's side!

The universe is expanding, encouraging us to expand our minds a bit, never know what you might find, but be sure it's more than you can dream of in your own philosophy. (Cribbed from Shakespeare's Hamlet!).

On Health and Hygine

Good health is natural.
Exercise sensibly,
   Drink sensibly,
     Eat sensibly.

Do not have bathroom scales in the home,
   or have a thermometer in the home,
     or have a medical dictionary in the home.

There you go...
And enjoy your health.
(Remember it's one of those things that money can't buy)
In other words don't let it become a pre-occupation, a worry; for that's only a fear taking on...

Hygiene, both personal and professional, is important, not only for the discomfort caused to others, it shows a lack of awareness and self respect...(reflecting our inner nature?)... it is said that 'cleanliness is next to godliness' – physical as well as mental- so what image are you showing the world about your inner self is the question... and despite the teachings of making none, people *do* make face value judgements!

On Spontaneity

Coming upon an idea that agrees with you, having put it in the box with your other truths, naturally, sooner or later you'll wish to share it. Be careful, use your own words. Don't just repeat what's been read or heard, because this is the path to dogma; of which there's too much in the world already. Please don't add to it, be spontaneous, every time you speak keep it simple using different words where possible; thus keeping discussions fresh and interesting; which will make *you* think about what you're saying too.

A big plus - it will help prevent you becoming boring! . Promise!

"It does not require many words to speak the truth*

* Chief Joseph, 1840 - 1904, Nez Perce tribe. Famously spoke in Washington D.C. to Congress about the native American Indians' experience after the coming of the white settlers.

On Certainty.

Certainty and safety as concepts are illusory. You cannot win an argument for there'll always be a resentment, because 'facts' do not exist – only opinions – formed by subjective interpretations. Safe from what? Safe from fear, the unknown, loss, yourself /others? If you want freedom from fear, then look at it and it will diminish; you'll know yourself better. Susan Jeffers wrote a whole book about feeling the fear and doing it anyway'.

As for 'safety' nothing comes from that, a life which is routine, unchallenged and certain is dull and grey; (the unexamined life that Socrates spoke of?) where's the *zest*, passion, the joys of colour?

"If you don't go out on a limb, you'll not get any fruit".

(U.S. President, Jimmy Carter).

Asking the Sage.

I asked the sage about life and death
He barely paused for breath in answering:
"My son you're looking for a bolt-hole for your soul
and I cannot offer one.
What can be said you don't already see,
what will you learn from eternity?
(which is not forever, in all honesty).
Anyway, nothing is what it seems
(be you awakened or in your dreams)
yet, you wish from me to hear
about that which you hold most dear.
Everything's negotiable is a sombre truth
Nothing's been discovered yet really idiot proof.
I cannot reveal what I do not know,
the rainbows, U.F.O.'s, crop circles are there to show
the future's uncertainty and there's nothing to fear.
With no truth to say what's true,
read the signs through an open mind...

Life's for going with the eternal flow,
or being left behind"
Which is the story of my years and age;
given time enough, you'll be your own sage.

The 'R' Words

Rules.

In the Realm of B4, that's to say before earthly birth, there's only spirit, nothing solid to touch. It's life, awareness, but only in theory so to speak. We are born. All different now, limited to only six senses; but Hey! Good to be here, or what?...For some purpose of why we're here, an aim, some do claim; but with a free will that can change the game.

W.H.Auden, the poet, suggested we're here to help the others, but what the others were here for he didn't know.   Yeah, right.

What about these limitations, a) the Laws of the Universe; b) mankind's mundane laws, rules, customs, commandments, protocols or social mores? They're to keep you in your place, the riff-raff out, protecting property above humanity, devised by the haves and their continued having; not yours you may be sure...

but that's o.k. 'cos we're not going to be bothered by them anyway, (the haves or the rules). Conform and die unto yourself.

Universal laws can't be dodged as they're bigger than you and are just the way things work. A philosopher a long time ago suggested laws should be based on principle only... That'll be the day. The other stuff is a reflection on how we co-exist and if you're willing to flout convention, you must also be willing to accept responsibility for your actions, because the majority will not understand and will condemn. In our raised awareness that's fine; 'cos no-one else is going to know about us anyway... and so, being invisible, as the Inca Shaman have it; we are free to change the world... to accomplish anything; and by letting others take the credit for it. *

- *Source – Shaman, Healer, sage by Alberto Villoldo Ph. D*

Reverberation!

The general assumption is that there was a 'Beginning', by either accident or design. An original breath of life from which has come all that's followed and all that's to come. The very first quiet, yet mighty reverberation gave cause to creation and eventually light; moving on through the evolutionary process from the first to final solution, where death and dissolution yields to birth and new days.

From tiniest atoms to the bigger than big cosmos, black holes holding in light until it's time for that lights' release; re-creating... overnight or longer term, yin and yang balances of the whole co-exist, for they are one and the same: a part of the whole.

What's gone before has yielded through an interaction of variances, evolutionary and or climactic; changes adapting to produce the latest crops and species. Question is... where are the fishes with feet still to come ashore, the so-called 'missing links'? Conventional wisdom agrees that moving from one form to another is a long slow process; so should we not see this in action, this evolution's activity, progress, natural selection?   Where's the link between apes and homo sapiens (man)?   There is none.

We are not descended from apes; humans are their own unique species, sub-divided into races, which are really only variations on a theme. None better or worse than the others; just different, adapted according to Nature, nurture and environment as required in order to continue our existence.

Evolution is a creative process that moves quickly! From one generation to the next... how can it not be so? If a species is to survive the fundamental law of 'Adapt or Die', the new information to cause the necessary change is in the mother's milk or equivalent in animal, insect, vegetable or mineral kingdoms. Which is why the dinosaurs died out, they couldn't adapt quickly enough to the last ice age.   Makes you think...consider 'superbugs' in hospitals.

There's eco-balance, many species have unique ways of dealing with extremes, in temperature, poisonous plants, mighty pressures deep in the oceans, or even thin air. If changes come then they must adapt again.

Life is one directional, creating variations to deal with circumstances or something entirely new; insects and plants have done / are doing better than most it seems, as botanists it seems continually demonstrate to us.

So – New creations evolve,   Evolution creates anew.

Ergo : Creation and Evolution are the *same thing* – Life's process!

Wow!

End of any more argument on that subject! (but probably not...).

Evolution like time is not a constant. Look up 'Cambrian explosion'. See that paleontology raises the question of possibly evolution being worked by differing 'rules' in earth's history and that many species depended on 'chance' environmental events, rather than simple adaptation over time.

Nothing is certain about the past either it seems.

Respect.

    Not too much respect about nowadays, respect for others' points of view, or lifestyles if different; or respect for nature and your own spirit. Slow down! If you're so busy rushing to be somewhere, other side of town or further up the greasy pole, there'll be so much being missed along the way.

    Somebody said we should 'take time to smell the roses'; in doing so you are in the 'moment' connecting to what's going on around and about   This smelling of roses is meant to be calming and invigorating at the same time adding a perspective to your activities and awareness in becoming a part of it all.

    If for any reason you're getting a hard time, someone shouting at you, just look 'em in the eye imagining him or her unclothed ... try not to laugh out loud and giving the game away ... or just say in and to yourself "I am in control here, of this situation... you do *not* want to know what I'm thinking..."Get the idea? You are cool and in command; after the tirade suggest how the problem may be resolved and that you're on it.

Of course to receive respect you first have to give some, so don't put yourself in the position of being thought of as something less than you'd like because of your own behaviour. It follows then to give respect you need respect yourself.   It's an aspect of love, as is taking time to be aware and a part of it all – this astounding universe that's carrying all before it... accept this, as we cannot see the big picture...

Allow time to accomplish your stuff, thus more time to think on.   Arrive at your appointments early so having a few minutes to watch and absorb what's going on. Traveling by train or bus, be early so as to see the birds on the rooftops or telegraph wires, the rainbow, traffic hurrying by (where are they all going?), vapour trails, clouds' silver linings... you name it.

Who knows, you may strike up a friendship at the station or bus stop; but not if no time is allowed for it!, if you are so focused on concerns; missing all of life going on around you on our lovely planet; the daisy or buttercup that's come up through a crack in the pavement or wall.   Doesn't that give a glow in your heart?   This is a wonderful world... If you don't think so, then a Big Point of Life is really being missed...it's here to be enjoyed. (I kid you not).

Observe; then feel a part of it, respecting yourself. Included in the umbrella word of Respect is a whole bunch of other R words, like Re-use, Reduce, Recycle; Rejection and Reception.

Are you beginning to get the idea that everything is Related and connected in someways? In terms of respect; respect the world we're in, (here before your coming and will be long after we're gone too).

Take home your litter, don't leave it for the cleaners to pick up, they've enough else to do without your adding to their workload. Recycle – well if and when we run out of resources, assuming (as some will have it) we are our own grand-children, then will you curse or bless your ancestors?

Rejection – is the most harmful experience to get from another human being, self-worth values go right out the window, plummeting, causing a lot of pain and anguish... so be receptive, as has been said elsewhere, we all got something to say and a right to be heard. Think about it, if you give two – three – five minutes time to listen; how much has it cost?

At 20 years of age how many minutes have you lived?... in that context a couple or a few ..is no time at all.

e.g.: Assume 24 hours a day, 365 days a year; that equals 525,600 minutes per year.

Therefore   20 yrs = 10,512,000 mins.

30 yrs = 15,768,000 mins.

40 yrs = 21,024,000 mins.

50 yrs = 26,280,000 mins, and so on.

Hard to argue that there's not enough time! Respect costs nothing then, really, does it?

"When you judge another you don't define them, you define yourself as some-one who needs to judge"... (Wayne Dyer)... to which I add – "and is lacking in respect".

Also consider that when you see another behaving in a way you cannot, do not judge them nor condemn; just thank him/her in your heart for showing you what you are not. Bless 'em and go on your way.

Relationships – At Work.

Do you always do as you're told? By whom and by what right? In doing what you're told you are in agreement with the 'teller', like it or not. Are you agreeing to grow, expand, be empowered; or are you willing to be limited; (which isn't in your best interest, is it?)

If you are Boss at workplace, how do you treat your staff, those that you're responsible to and for. Are you helping them be better, or do you stand on their shoulders, shouting all day? How are feelings at end of the day...exhilarated that requirements were achieved, all going home happy, ready to have a good evening with the family... or dog tired, frustrated, angry because it's all so difficult and draining of energy. Are you expanding or limiting... how is your Boss with you and workmates?

Point is, that in helping others you helps* yourself. viz: reaping what you sow, the company you work for does too.

*(helps – plural as this is ongoing, more than once, yes?)

Look at what you do, asking how can I help. Prepare to be surprised at the answers and results they bring when put into practice.   Cosmos is expanding, why try to limit that which cannot be limited? Must be something to do with Ego, I'd guess.

Relationships – Sex

This is a topic we as a species have a lot of problems with...

Lots of taboos about sex... just don't go there; o.k? No need for taboos. The purpose of sex is very simple – it's a celebration of love; a beautiful expression of love which will eventually bring procreation, a celebration of another kind of love   Sex isn't really 'making love'.

Love is all about intimacy, yes, but a whole lot more, including trust, vulnerability, honesty and sharing with another; which is why *loving* sex is a celebration.

However, there's a dark side – lust and 'sexploitation'.   For many, sex is a commodity, like food and money, a whole 'industry' dealing in it.

For some sex is a spectator sport and advertisers know well that sex 'sells', but really the above are only forms of lust or titillation; which has nothing to do with sex's real and loving intention.

Sex acts can become obsessive or addictive; addictions are always substitutes for goodness only knows what, but are unhealthy for mind, body and spirit.

Not any more to be said about that really.

Just remember, love carries with it some pain and true love will overcome this pain.   Just another of life's paradoxes.

Relationships – Love.

    Lovers in my life, were there to show me something I didn't wish to know, that true love's always a letting go. For when what's desired doesn't return, was never really mine; but then...what did I know; in youthful unconcern did I love many loves and did so yearn. Loves returning I was learning was really a minor score; the ensuing freedom is in the setting free, you free yourself furthermore. Better to have loved some and lost than never loved at all, but then having freedom to love again; and more!

Relationships – People.

"The more I have to do with people, the more I like my cat"

(on a 'fridge magnet).

You have relationships with all you meet even if only ever once – maybe or maybe not leaving a lasting impression, or have a lasting impression left you. Possibly have forgotten him/her/them in five minutes; the opposite holds true too, naturally.

People relationships are all about how one interacts, something that can't be done in front of television or computer; to really connect at some point you needs good eye contact. Eyes are windows to the soul and if you can't look people honestly in the face (shifty-eyed) then you got a problem that you'd best look into... I know, bad pun... others will stay away and not be happy in your company. Mind, that's not the worst; there's others who when making eye contact you can't help feeling though the lights are on, there's nobody home.

Maybe you've met a few like that.

What's happening is their soul has gone walkabout, or if you like, is sitting on their shoulder because it's not happy with the egocentric lifestyle; so when they re-engage with the rest of us (by not thinking about themselves so much), then you can communicate again.

We need to go to market, rubbing shoulders with the princes and paupers, because in not doing so, you can get 'above' yourself or become isolated and insular. All the gunmen who have shot up High Streets or schools were loners; living in some dreamed up fantasy ending in disaster; *on their own.*

There's the expression 'you should get out more' which is what this is all about.   Balance.   Shops and clubs help with this and you'll help others in their balance whether realized or not.   Talking ideas through will answer the unasked questions; so you'll stay sane, whatever *that* word means.

We are a people planet, seven billion of us and counting, not getting on too well internationally though are we? To change high level relationships we need have good relations at lower levels, right down to family, friends and neighbours. Stands to reason, as pretty much all the dictators and feudal lords who've mis-ruled countries were not in any kind of stable relationship, no yin to their yang, that is, *balance,* whether married or not.

Ideally relationships are supportive and nurturing, when you need a shoulder to cry on, and when you don't; playful. Lovely word that: full of play; sounds like fun. Growing old through time's relentless march is o.k., but young in spirit, not 'growing up', is more o.k.

One of today's ills is technology. Society is high tech – low touch, has become a lottery, looky me, all form and no feelings or substance world. So no to on-line shopping, it's not in your interest as a person, you need sales assistants who are really interested in helping; not thinking about their commission; but you, the customer. (More about this in the chapter on money).

Sit down and write a letter to someone you've not seen in a while just to let 'em know you're thinking of him/her. Picture postcards are brilliant for this 'cos there's only 3 and a bit square inches (about 8cm) in which to write a message, like about 22 words!; so how hard can that be?, but the impact it'll have is so much more than e-mail; and is because *yourself* has handled the card; wrote in your own hand and even licked the stamp... it's personal with your good energy all over it. Meanwhile e-mail and texts are quite soulless; good for what they are, quick communications, but regardless of wording, hasn't got any of *you* in it. Vibes, man.

Why is it when looking at a best friend you wish to be more like they are, making you feel good whatever, even when they know you ain't so perfect, still liking you anyway? My own definition of best friends is of one who you can never impose on. This is in feelings, not necessarily ever talked about between friends; only ever get three or four in a lifetime and not all at the same time; so watch out!

Equally, when you don't call when there's troubles, you'll soon be told off for not doing so.

Bless 'em; they're treasure beyond counting.

Life is uncomplicated, it just goes on. Mankind has made life very hard for many through manipulations of all kinds, in the need to control that which needs no controlling. Out of dissatisfactions are the needs to be superior in some way;

The expression 'of having an attitude problem' means that the attitude does not conform to the controller's notion, so one has to be brought into line.

Oh dear.

When free in your heart you cause problems for those who are not free in theirs', abiding by rules, not liking your non-conformity – you're an anarchist* of course. Mankind needs more mild subversives, Ruby Tuesdays; blowing away this 'conventional wisdom' thing.

- *Anarchy : from the Greek anarkhos = without chief or ruler.* Think for yourself; nothing to do with terrorism or paranoia.

Really, the greatest gift for anyone is to leave them alone!

Doing this from a loving perspective results in no fear, try it, you'll see.

I have in my head the opening pages of a story about what it'd be like if some cataclysm caused all the satellites spinning in our heavens to be ejected into Space, or to fall into the seas... no sat.nav., cell phones, tv, internet, on-line banking, nor spies in the skies... we go back 100+ years!

How would we react during the time it would take to put the satellites back up there again, with no precious toys to play with, (or more likely being ruled by!)?   Respond out of insecurity, or would it be strange at first, but then managing fine? Why do we need faster and yet faster 'thingummies', apart from the fact someone somewhere is making a lot of money, I suspect.

Governments would be in a pickle, unable to control or spy on us in their democratic or dictatorial paranoia. Everything would slow down for a while and isn't that an interesting thought in itself... as John Lennon urged us: . Imagine!

And no, I'm not saying it was better in the 'good old days' but so much is taken for granted as 'progress' that needs challenging from time to time; help keep a balance (That word again!)

Relationships – Food.

Another topic with marked extremes – anorexia and obesity. While millions don't have enough food to be able to make that choice. Many don't even have clean water to drink. Abject poverty. There is more than enough food to go around in the world, 'Make Poverty History' campaigns will never succeed without leadership from governments with the necessary political will.

Food is a commodity, the giant corporate businesses along with market exchanges demand their percentages; while all the time the system is about said governments keeping the world safe for commerce. How then *can* anything change meaningfully?... meanwhile, how are you faring? (No pun intended).

Respect your food; bless it before eating more slowly, allowing digestive processes to have a chance to work. Let all of you as well as tummy enjoy what you're taking in. Don't eat with your eyes either... which means not looking at the next forkful while mouth is still full... In eating more slowly you'll get into a balance, probably eat less, maybe helping with any weight issues you have.

Being in the moment, enjoying the experience of savouring what is really fuel for the body. You are after all what you eat; think about it... taking drugs (prescribed or otherwise), more than enough alcohol at any one time, have 'side effects' – so why not food? – it's ingested, and with all the dubious ingredients in prepared and packaged food-stuffs found in the shops nowadays.

<u>Mood Food</u>

Eating when stressed doesn't help deal with the stress; have a hot drink instead, 'a good ole 'cuppa rosy' as they so often did in those 1950's British films. Hot drinks move endorphins around the brain – avoiding the other three brain cells I hope! – and helps keep moods 'up'

"I ask that this food be blessed, that the fruits of the earth feed and nourish my physical body; the blessing feed my spiritual body. I thank all those involved in bringing this food to my table'. Amen

Relationships – Money.

Oh dear. This is the big one.

Let me tell you about money... Money is nothing!

Excuse me? Sorry to have to repeat this: money is nothing.It's only bits of cheap metal and coloured scrip. It's not what it is, it's what it represents and what you can do with it. Of itself, it's well... nothing.

Nowadays money has been caught up in the digital revolution, computer generated having even less substance than scrip, but still manages to appear in your bank accounts as debt! It is not real, the money, nor, by logical argument is the debt.

To help you get over the shock, here's a story –

Once upon a time work was done, a service provided or goods supplied; your neighbour would offer a token of appreciation which would be a barter or indeed cash. All very civilized. Adventurers came home from afar with all sorts of must have consumables, but at a price; and thereby was commerce.

Goods followed by services or labour became commodities now charged for. In early 13th century the then Church changed the ruling on usury, because up until then charging interest was frowned upon; the time between loan and repayment date was God's and so... usury was downgraded to 'excessive interest' without being clear on what excessive meant. How convenient.

Naturally the churches, kings and robber barons became very interested...(excuse me, another pun).

Money became a commodity like everything else and banks came into being, time followed in this vein; standardized through the industrial revolution, manufactories and capitalism. As slavery died out *wages* slavery was born.

Personnel, workforces, staff are now designated 'human resources'. All this justified in the name of 'profit' and 'growth' measured in monetary terms – yet still enterprises go 'bust' – and all with it the ugliness of greed which allows billions of souls to live on a dollar a day; while in the other corner, billionaires... extremes; and another imbalance.

Where do you find yourself in relation to money? Do you have enough or not, and how much is 'enough' anyway? You can only know this for your own self, but there's the universal law of attraction at work here and in relation to money, it is :'the more you chase after it, the more it runs away from you! If money is your god, getting into 'get rich quick' schemes, gambling, lotteries and suchlike; you will never be rich. Sorry but it's true. Actually you are more likely to die in the week than to win the Big Draw!

The original purpose of money was to enable exchange and as a reward given (the token of appreciation), rather than demanded... which is the key to the whole money mystery. Easier for a rich man to pass through a camel than to enter the kingdom – or something like that – 'what should I do to be saved?' was asked of Jesus; 'give up all you have and follow me – not in a literal sense – but do as I do, the love of money being the root of all evil'. So Jesus was maybe saying money is nothing.

Entering the kingdom means raising awareness and self's enlightenment in letting go of need. Life is how you deal with it, attitude; starting within yourself and money is a part of that life.

Another story to help explain –

Imagine one day waking up to find yourself out of work .Everyone else too. Even if previously unemployed, are now equal with all others; point being we all have to apply for the job / career / vocation that *really* is what you want to do, forever. It's well known that most of those in work hate their jobs... why? Because they're only doing it for the money! And it's never enough, even with overtime. So in   squaring this particular circle; question yourself about what work you really want to do, regardless of pay scale; what will get you up in the morning looking forward to the workday, especially on Monday mornings?   Well, whatever it is, that's what you 'should' be doing, because love now enters the equation.

If you're good enough there's room for one more and everyone at the workface is loving every minute of it... I tell you money is no longer an issue, money has become the by-product of your activity.   Likely we'd all be earning full time wages for part time hours!

It's this energy thing, of which more about in a later chapter.

Hate job = negativity and resistance.

Love job = positively moving mountains.

All rather fanciful I hear you thinking, but just for yourself, promised success at the outset, what would you do? (Why aren't doing it anyway... ?) Loving what you do, your project will be successful; sure, some hiccups along the way, obstacles becoming challenges to deal with, stepping stones towards the end.

No such thing as failure. Work then is no longer seen as such, it's a game and fun; think of workstation as 'play'station.   Now we're talking!

Energy will rise, weight off shoulders, smiling a lot more, on good terms with all you meet because you have enough.   Probably less than you'd imagine right now, but that doesn't mean you won't be rich; you're balanced and more aware and life's a peach. Stop *chasing* money – it's nothing! Being rich is a relative term. Doing what you love while loving what you do is then being who you are. Crucial.

About 'enoughness' – consider in you, you are enough and you'll not need more.

Believing you're not enough, means you will always be wanting more.*

If you measure success in monetary terms only, try thinking of true success as being a sense of satisfaction and fulfillment; (which of course it is).

Having time for family, friends, yourself, walking the dog, singing, writing, painting, playing; all those happy things and concepts which are real, yet funny in they have nothing to do with money.

Ben Franklin said that 'time is money'. Actually time is more important than money; and time doesn't exist! (according to quantum theory, at least).

People who have time for others are rich, they have a wealth of appreciation from others. Many lonely people out there longing for someone to talk to, ask your doctor or the Samaritans, they can tell you; beyond which, people want to be heard, be listened to... don't you? And that takes time.

Also think what you might also learn because everyone knows something. In giving others a chance to be heard, saying little yourself is a form of healing...

because the problem will usually get talked out, given time.

This is empoweringful, (a word I like and made up).

Sure, plenty of professionals out there, but they have this 50 minute hour...must be something to do with money I suppose.

Have time for others, whoever they may be; see how much you gain.

- *Thanks to Marisa Peer for this insight, which I have 'proved' to be true.*

Fearweather Friends.

Hid away in their ivory towers
Abusing position and assumed powers
Mealy – mouthed, grasping and unkind;
In our beautifully coloured world
Little grey suits with little grey minds.
Usurers wanting to count the money,
Only if it is their own.
Preying on your uncertainties,
Fearweather friends with some small piece
Of peace of mind, to you they'll sell.
Commissioning scrip even they can't spend.
Amassing possessions as their notion of heaven,
Forgetting they don't get to take it with them...
Except maybe to hell.

Relationships – More on Success.

Here's a story – years ago I saw on tv, a race in the Olympics, in it the world record was broken.

The athlete who came in 8th and last had achieved her personal best time, never run faster.   She was over the moon with excitement, to have been a competitor in a race where records were broken…to her it was fantastic!

You can do only your best and sure there'll be others quicker, (so what?), enjoy and celebrate your own achievements and successes as well as those of the world champion; there's only one of 'em at a time.

Loser for coming in last in the race? ..Don't think so, failure and success are mirages; not always what they claim or appear to be. Enjoy accomplishments. Be satisfied.

Worthy.

Honest.

<u>Results</u> – How to Achieve #1

Do what in your own mind 'should' be done; not that which you'd 'like' to do. After a while you'll find what you'd 'like' to do is in fact what you 'should' be doing anyway!

This is how to achieve, getting things done, if ultimately you're to be mover and shaker.

<u>Results</u> – How to Achieve #2

Each day promise yourself to do 'one thing' that's important to you no matter what. Unimportant how big or small the task, or even if it only takes two minutes. Just make sure to do this 'one thing'. When reviewing the day and all that's happened, if the 'one thing' was done/ achieved/ dealt with; it was a successful day for you! Only one thing.

Say "well done" to your spirit and thank it. Just the one, don't get greedy; It follows then that all your days will be satisfactory at least. You bet.

Resistance.

"Resistance is futile'   (The Borg).

Just a reminder about the Law of Attraction: what you focus on you draw to you... What you resist, persists for this very reason; don't give the adversary a hand-hold to come back at you with. This is what is meant by the biblical advice of turning the other cheek. Also, if you take up the weapon of your enemy you become like him... So in gaining victory over other men be strong; but in gaining victory over yourself, (by not resisting) you become powerful.

Well there's a thought.

I like these short chapters... how are you doing so far?

Religion.

'The religion of one age is the literary entertainment of the next'

(Ralph Waldo Emerson)

'Truth in matters of religion is simply the opinion that has survived'

(Oscar Wilde)

Hundreds of religions have come and gone.

Even the Sun and Moon have been our gods; the ancients from Greece, Rome, Egypt had all sorts of deities and customs, swept away by events and time. In the same way too in future times today's cherished faiths will be overtaken by others; in whatever new form they may be.

So what price does the 'one true god' come down to? Consider there's only one God, having many, many names, dependant on place and time and culture. As to whether this matters... probably it's not beliefs so much as what is done with them... So no it shouldn't matter. Except of course, for the great banana skin of life where some folk actually think they're better than the likes of thee and me. And it's always 'important' people who do much harm to others, have you ever noticed?

If you have a personal sense of moral code, of how you deal with others, how you see yourself in the light of this code that you may or may not adhere to strictly; then surely this is your own religion and within that framework, *You* are your own god. So from that perspective, one doesn't need a church...you're walking around in one!

Typical dictionary definitions for 'religion' include – 'practice of religious beliefs, ritual observances of faith, beliefs concerning the cause and purpose of the Universe, especially when considered as the creation of a superhuman agency; usually involving devotions and ritual observances, often containing a moral code on the conduct of human affairs'.

Interesting to note the term 'superhuman agency' in the above – isn't it funny how God is seen as a bigger version of ourselves?, with all the frailties judgements and hang-ups down here on earth. Why would any God be limited to merely being superhuman? Look at the universe in all it's ever expanding incredible vastness; at the other end of the scale the minuteness of particles, which is even more incredible. Whether this was all created or is happenstance; it's merely down to some superhuman agency? And so God is made in the image of Man!

Albert Einstein, a great thinker said he didn't try to imagine a personal god, he felt it enough to stand in awe of the structure of the world ...Had he sat still for a while and silenced the ego as much as he could, he'd have discovered deeper inside a 'small voice' ... call it intuition, inner wisdom conscience, awareness or spirit, call it whatever you wish to; it's within you and reflected outside you:

'And what is good, Phaedrus

And what is not good –

Need we ask anyone to tell us these things?' (Socrates)

How much more would Albert have stood in awe, in this, his personal religion?　For that is really what it is.

You can do this too. it's meditation, in your inner heart in time you'll come to realize, to intuition, a knowing of your own of that which is good. Go on, no-one else will ever know for it's your link to your own personal God. Yes, Albert, yours too.

I know, mention meditation and eyes roll in sockets – 'hippy new age stuff, 'no thank you' - meditation is not that; it's not what you do, it's what you allow to happen by being in a quiet mind in a quiet place; just that.

Whole books writ large on this subject only to tell you that.

See how you gets on (plural, remember), that's the challenge – face up to yourself and see what's inside... simple enough but not always easy, you'll have to work at it a bit, not for hours, ten minutes to start with can bring results - and you'll be looking at you from heart's eyes point of view.

"When you are with someone you love very much, you can talk and it is pleasant, but the reality is not in the conversation. It is simply being together.

Meditation is the highest form of prayer. In it you are so close to God that you don't need to say a thing – it's just great to be together".

(Swami Chetananda).

The word God in any language has lost much of it's meaning; throughout all history God has been hi-jacked for everyone by those with hidden agendas; with proofs and convictions as to definition, identity and of course 'His will'. As an individual pre-disposed to a Creator or Divine source of some kind – certain themes religious, philosophical or spiritual will maybe strike a chord with you; thus you grow in your understandings of this Divinity.

Or possibly your perceptions are those held since childhood.

If you are not so disposed then certain themes scientific, mechanical or evolutionary will strike a chord in you; thus you grow in understanding the nature of things.   You may hold views a bit from each camp; living on our restricted to three dimensional, apparently solid physical world, we cannot see the big picture; or indeed if there even is one.   Is this not the basis of religion and science?

Religion and Churches.

"We do not need churches, because they will teach us to quarrel about God".

(Chief Joseph).

Beliefs are personal and individual, which churches don't like. By churches I mean the institution of organized religion; not necessarily any particular parish or priest (by any name), but the industry that seems to have always been around and from ages past.

When religion is attacked the attackers are missing the point that religion is nothing to do with churches! Church is only interested in power and the Establishment... All wars have been 'holy wars' have they not? Or jihads or crusades or simply 'just wars' (surely an oxymoron)... Blessed are the peacemakers...

As for inquisitions and penalties extorted for heresy, even if, (or especially?) one is not a follower of the faith in question.   Churches to this day conceal truth failing mankind because they're a part of the system of their country and have become politicized, gaining a taste for power, the designs of the bishops become 'God's will'... expediency more like... and don't they just love all their secrets?

The institution of churches has no interest in advancing mankind – look at the Christian Dark age – 600+ years of the dead hand of authority keeping the peasants and serfs in their place and in fear. Later in the Middle Ages when science was finding it's feet, questioning the understanding of the times; what was the Church's response? Amongst others ask Copernicus and Galileo.

So it follows that a church as an institution is interested in self perpetuation   No prophet started any church, they came into being long after the prophet's death or claimed ascendancy; via disciples and writings following at a much later time.

An institution, referring to any dictionary is – 'an organization founded for religious, educational, scientific or social function'.   The adjective institutional – of, in, or like an institution, *regimented and / or unimaginative.* (my italics).

So does any of this matter?   Only if it does to you. Research and come up with your own truth; letting it set you free... in doing so you'll allow everyone else the same freedom.   If their truth is different, so what?

"Dear god save me from your followers"   (Car bumper sticker).

On Sundays.

On Sundays we go to our temples
'saving' money on special offers,
filling the superstore's coffers
when we could be 'saving' ourselves.
Don't you see all the whiles,
this congregation only smiles –
As seen on tv.!

Reasoning.

It would seem in the Beginning is the System; containing state/church/news/media/advertising and other interested parties telling us what's Right and Proper and what to believe. It ain't necessarily so.

There's always another way to look at things and with nothing to prove, no need to start a New Movement. Down the years have been some great thinkers, men (and too few women) whose works have advanced our understanding of Mankind's place in the scheme of it all a few more tentative steps.

Science has also contributed to our knowledge discovering more about the building blocks of nature and her workings. Once metaphysics and physics were much the same thing, overlapping occasionally... but as quantum's world shows, these two branches are closing together again, even if reluctantly.

Philosophy has many schools of expression in which our activities are examined including the nature of reality of being, the principles of reasoning, ethics and even the mind. Also looking into the use of language, politics, art, religion and so on.

The categories have funny names (from which I spare you), our philosophy is homespun, which means simple and uncomplicated. All very interesting you may say, how does that butter my parsnips?, a lot of this stuff is over my head; some subjects are really too 'dry'. Yes, I know.

All philosophers it seems, even those over 1000+ years past were straight jacketed by universities...! They're part of the system... though to be fair, a number of worthies fought the system from within. Bless 'em.

Probably at times you've thought nothing much is certain, that you only know what is from own experience. If something makes you happy it must then be all right. Maybe. It's occurred to you that if you can't think it, it can't exist or the other way around, if you can think it, it must therefore be possible.

These are just a few concepts called philosophical... the difference between Socrates, Russell and yourself/myself is that whilst we're able to think stuff; they were able to express their ideas well, but often in a language not easily understood by the likes of you and me. But that's o.k. because one day we'll catch up.

How about we all travel the same path at once? I doubt the road would be wide enough. Don't follow a signpost just 'cos it says This Way, there's other ways to go; to experience, depending on your awareness doing as you'd be done by; or not, stumbling along your chosen path, not in any hurry to go someplace. Happy, for any old road will take you nowhere, depending which sign you follow and the level you set your happiness dial.

The road to innermost feelings is a good place to start from, how much left in the dark is down to you... but remember it only takes a candle to break even the darkest night... how's your light?

So far so good. Now, what's the best way to deal with life, the universe and everything else, in the still young 21st century?

Quick fix answer – Throw the tv out the window!

This is not as radical as might be thought at first. I challenge anybody to put telly away for a mere 168 hours and when reviewing the week, see if you missed it all that much. 90% of those accepting the challenge will find it's not missed at all!.

No kidding. You don't need it. There's so much more fun to be had not watching the idiot lantern. Why?... well, all the interminable mediocre prima donnas masquerading as quality; (not to mention some really scary people on the minority channels); all with their shock-horror catalogues of disasters and gloom, rumours of wars, incessant advertising / 'game shows' reality(?) progs /brainwashing / conditioning that makes up the schedules, then repeated endlessly. Who needs it?

Not anyone with more than three and a half brain cells, I imagine.

If you cannot do without telly ask yourself why. You are not living yours, but someone else's dream, viz: programme makers and producers with their 'ideals'. When you do give it up... and it's easier than giving up smoking... suddenly all this free time needs taking up with... well, what? And that's a whole big question; being a free agent thinking objectively; discovering the new life after death you didn't know you were living. Brave new world!

But seriously, telly has become big brother of Orwellian proportions and conditioning, when free of it you'll understand this in your own way.

Go and support your local football club or knitting circle or any other sports or social club that appeals, never mind walking the dog! Not watching footy on the box is a better way to live; standing on the terraces or touchline, get the whole atmospherics, relate to the teams and see the game through your own eyes without some commentator colouring your vision for you.

Are you getting out of bed saying "great, another day to enjoy", when looking in the mirror while brushing teeth, winking at your reflection, asking "well, how many hearts you going to break today?"   No breakfast tv or radio before setting the tone for your day!

Next thing of course you'll discover giving up newspapers, as mostly they're about what's on the box anyway; and we're no longer interested in that, are you? You'll find out. No, really.

An unexpected bonus after dumping tv; not to mention sky-box, digi-box, d.v.d. player and half a mile of wiring, is when furniture is re-arranged, how everything *fits*.   More room space, plus no dead eye staring out of the corner. Comfortable

"I get all the news I need on the weather report" Paul Simon.

(in his song 'The Only Livin' Boy in New York')

Change is a Constant.

All is motion and resonance, therefore changes.

With each new learning the more realization of how much there is yet to know; enough for several lifetimes. Ergo – beware of experts. There are certainly leading authorities in all walks of life who are accomplished...but don't let them fool you they're expert, with definitive answers.

Once was thought atoms the smallest thing in creation and that the world was flat. Keep an open mind, not to the rightness of a theory, but to the possibility of the new idea, until the next one comes along – as it will – to challenge and replace (or not); so we think again, maybe.

It's the shock of the new keeps us on our toes, reminding us we are alive and can only be certain of uncertainty; comfort zones should always be challenged boundaries pushed against, as is the Universe's boundary, always and forever.

Wow! Changes are constantly happening...

Artists.

Artists are brave are they not?

Putting their work on view inviting criticism or praise; living in other's judgements of their efforts, while beauty is in the eye of the beholder. All such views are subjective, relative to the critic's understanding and experience; if the object is at all controversial... well, there's the open-ness of the reviewer to new concepts and ideas...

Safety Valve – Let it Go

We are limited to three dimensions in this earthly plane.

In the next, are there four primary colours, another dimension to length, breadth, height; another frame beyond past, present and future?

Cannot tell, but does it matter anyway? There's other levels of existence; accept it and let it go... just maybe everything *is* possible. You see, this way there's no pressure, no weight to carry around and thus living without constraint you'll discover it's the only way to be...and so life itself is the ultimate antidote to life!

Nuggets of Reasoning.

All truth passes through three stages:
First it is ridiculed
Second it is violently opposed
Third it is accepted as self evident
                          Arthur Schopenhauer.

First they laugh at you
Then they fight you
Then you win.
                          Mahatma Gandhi.

All truths begin as blasphemies.
                    George Bernard Shaw.

The reverse side also has a reverse side.
                        Japanese proverb.

A great truth is a truth whose opposite is also a great truth.
                              Neils Bohr.

Before you speak ask yourself is it kind, is it necessary,
Is it true and does it improve on the silence?
> Sathya Sai Baba.

Never let a sense of morals get in the way of doing what's right.
> Isaac Azimov.

We are all born children. The trick is how to remain one.
> Pablo Picasso.

A great teacher is one who practices what he preaches...
and may preach very little, if at all.
> Julia Cameron.

Laughter chases the devil away.
> Sonia Choquette.

I am the child of my past, I am the parent of my future.
> Anon.

Two roads diverged in a wood, and I took the one less traveled by. And that has made all the difference.
> Robert Frost.

Gold – Plated Rule.

Judge not or be the fool,
Everything is cool;
Unless it's not –
Then it's hot –
Ice burns or puts out the flame.
I proclaim the 'gold-plated' Rule –
Everything is Cool.

Responsibility.

A situation has come about that needs attention - somebody needs to act, i.e. take responsibility.
If not you, who   Then... if not now... when?

King and Clown.

When i am a king,
Oh! my heart, it sings!
... but when i am a clown
i let myself down
and with all humanity,
who are relying on me
... i do not love me enough
it seems
to realize the dreams
of everyone;
and myself.

The 'F' Word.

Everything is born of love or a lacking in love; the ultimate lack is fear. Why does anyone do anything...? It's because they are acting out a belief based In love or fear. Fear causes stress, which is a killer, a primary cause of illnesses, which can be lost deep within the psyche, as well as obvious, the unresolved stress, that is.

Where does fear come from? It is acquired, subconsciously a lot of the time, lodged in the memory; and thus when a situation re- activates the memory and associated fear, it stops you dead in you tracks, and you don't know why...

Falsehood Expressed As Reality – that's the answer.

Imagined as well as real. Imagined fears are ridiculous because they truly are not real; except of course they *feel* very real. Feelings and emotions are very much what this is all about. Feelings in your gut and heart is where all truths are held; if your truths are based in lies, well, there's a conflict within, no wonder people are depressed or worse.

You wonder about evil. Folk do strange things, not rational acts of violence or abuse, stemming from an idea held about themselves, an idea which is fearful.

Ask "what do you think you're doing?" of someone, who maybe knows it's a 'wrong' thing in question; but in their own eyes or mind it's o.k.... not hating themselves for being 'bad' or a 'monster', because *they* don't see themselves as anything other than 'normal'. Ask anybody to describe normal and they'll describe themselves; of course they will!

Suppose you smoke 10 ciggies a day, which you see as normal. 20 a day would therefore be excessive, but if you're a 20 a day man, that would be normal. What is 'normal' other than a yardstick to value or judge something by, subjectively.

If you cannot handle the fear then neuroses and psychoses set in, needing to to be dealt with in love; not drugs, with counseling from love also. No 'snap out of it' approach, nor psychobabble, or to use a coping mechanism... who wants to just *cope* with troubles, why not deal with them, getting out from under; and be a bit more carefree.

Plato said to trust no-one who hadn't 'been there', so choose your counselor wisely.

Another aspect to consider is conscience. You have one in that you've a moral code of your own. Lacking conscience is fear; lacking feelings is fear, both forms of denial as to one's own spirituality. The whole fear thing works both ways, acting out of fear, or hiding away from it, with or without conscience; a not taking responsibility for yourself.

The blame culture of today is all about that, keeping your fears down and out of sight, out of mind.

'Rememberances' – (as antidotes for life, after the tv is out the window).

You can never win an argument.
Best to avoid extremes.
Be spontaneous, in the moment, aware, while living your owned dreams; not thinking about yourself too much.
Rules are for everyone else doing the best they can within those limitations.
In living and letting live, there is no 'them'.
Money is nothing.
Be playful and nurture relationships.
Nothing to be a'feared of.
Life is absurd.
Everything is Cool.

Spooky Stuff No. 1 (Quantum).

The General Theory of Relativity allows light to travel at 186,282mps, And it has been thought for over 100 years that nothing can go faster. Well, recent scientific developments have found a sub-atomic particle faster than light! So, maybe what that means is light can't travel faster than light; this particle whatever it 's called is not light, but some other energy... This puts spanners amongst the pigeons... a whole new change of view, pushing the frontiers back again; we can only wonder at what will be discovered next.

Don't you just love it? What's been true may not be anymore; the uncertainty principle strikes again! This doesn't cause you a problem does it? I mean, we're all in this together. Maybe this will help:-

E = everything else, made from evolution or creation /time/ uncertainty.

Our 3 dimensional existence gives us triangles; remember the speed/ distance /time version?, using that principle one gets variations of Energy being equal to evolution/creation multiplied by time, divided by uncertainty; or any of the other combinations...

Well, it's a thought.

There's something new discovered daily if the Press are to be believed, the basis for modern scientific thinking (and possibly now, a shaky one at that), is, $E = mc^2$; probably most famous and least understood equation.

Never mind, consider the possibilities this has given rise to since; such as in cosmology.   There's anomalies in gravity behaviour explained through Dark Matter, which is both invisible and un-measurable!! Apparently it's also accountable for 80% of all matter in existence, the 20% balance being 'ordinary' matter... which *can* be seen and measured.

There's a whopping great Unknown 'out there'... our friend Albert felt it enough to stand in awe at the structure of the world; Neils Bohr around at the time said that if you're not shocked at quantum theory you don't understand it.   Don't be shocked, be excited; the possibilities of, well... everything, are well... infinite! Phew!

There are other strange goings on: consider ten or eleven dimensions to the Universe shown to be; through supergravity and string theories and very difficult sums; while muddying the waters is entanglement.

It's getting into metaphysics a bit, basically when particles have bumped into each other they go on sharing their 'properties' (energy, mass, space and time), even from opposite sides of outer space, simultaneously!. At what would appear to be much faster than the speed of light squared; thought impossible... again paradox in distance no object.

This entanglement, as it's known, is understood to be going on all the time everywhere; it may yet be discovered working at more than just the microscopic level.

Then there's the Observer Effect, which is, that when you look to see something not there, it appears! The effect of observation *causes* virtual to become actual; it also seems that if the observer in an experiment is looking for a particular result, he influences the outcome to just that! Mind over matter using will to produce or materialize an effect...

Physics and metaphysics worked alongside each other one time, long ago, but moved apart in the last few centuries, though now seem to be coming together again. A Persian philosopher, Ibn Sina, better known in the West as Avicenna, a thousand years ago, without the help of quantum theory proposed that man through his imagination and thoughts (which are energies too) may be co-creators of our world and heresy of course in those days, probably to some, still is.

The Principle of Uncertainty shows us that measuring aspects of particles can't be nailed down; there's always room for doubt. At a more mundane level, the older and more experienced I am, the more am less confident of certainties... must be in tune to something then... if you go through life with fixed ideas, sure of everything; you in fact know nothing; for does not the tree bend with the wind (and winds of change?)

Stuff of science and the natural world is presented here simply to demonstrate the whole lot of mystery, which when solved reveals more mysteries...

Spooky Stuff No. 2 (Tao).

There is the Tao.

Tao Te Ching* is How Things Work.

The Tao claims all things rise from it, and rules by not ruling (not interfering), when nothing is done, nothing is left undone.

It talks of empty spaces... as in a clay pot; it's the space within that makes it useful; cut doors and windows into a room, it's the spaces again that are of use.   So you gain from what is there while usefulness comes from what's not there!

Space is required for things to exist but equally space needs a space of it's own, a quantum field; in order to exist itself.   This is the Tao, Spirit, Awareness, Matrix, Brahma, God, Manitou, Allah, Cosmic Consciousness or any other name you wish.

Consider fishes in shoals never bumping into each other and changing direction together; flocks of birds flying in harmony, not colliding – how is that?

They all share the same information simultaneously – all knowing what's where and when. In the same way in us humans every cell in you knows what every other cell knows and is experiencing; it's where mind resides – throughout all of you. Everything is an energy and information exchange...

How things work!

- *Pronounced Dow tay Jing.*

Enlightenment.

Very mis-understood word! What it really means is that one is *aware* of what's going on; aware of forces at work you have no control over. These forces are energies, pos and neg interacting as energy does; and also forces that you can and do have control over and are aware of consciously – and you practice this control.

Things are the way they are because that's just the way it is (the Tao?),

No use fighting it, the Universe is so much bigger than you! No, enlightenment is in accepting with detachment, what is, thereafter deciding what you wish to change, doing that, for example by engaging in affirmations, as the 'new-agers' have it; prayer as the religios have it and right action as the Buddhists have it and so on.

All without judgement. By engagement of the power of positive thinking, the power of now, the power of forgiveness, the power of intent, the power of the universal laws. All these things you do subconsciously anyway.

Enlightenment is in the being of Awareness, a wee bit alive to what the heck you're doing; in alignment with the Cosmic Mind, via your higher self, which lives in your heart of hearts and recognizing no limits.

The troubles of this present world are due to limitations; 'not alloweds', 'thou shalt nots' and suchlike. Churches limit God do they not? Governments and other Authorities limit their peoples, do they not? doing so only 'cos they're limited themselves; unable to see theirs' and therefore others' potential; thereby everything carries on just the same as ever was. History continually repeating itself... the human condition...full on.

You gets (plurals again) little help from the very authority that's set up to help you... and because those employees are working to scale and unhappy in their work they take it out on their customers, who are powerless to do other than grin and bear it. It's the way the System works; prime consideration is in self-perpetuation. The individual is given up (sacrificed?) to the Alter of Conformity, of job's worth, etc. Nothing much happens, bonuses paid out for least amount done, political masters congratulating themselves with honours and other trinkets, on their mis-management of the economy or war or whatever; no matter what.

Never mind, the new Aquarian age of enlightenment heralded via 2012's winter solstice is easing in and the signs of change and unrest globally in political and economic arenas are being felt. So, be a part of it all, vote NO! Vote Enough! Vote Sanity! Vote 'with your feet' (i.e. not voting) if have to!

Sign every petition. Let your voice be heard. But If change is to come and common sense returned to; if it doesn't start *with you*; who, what, where and when *does* it start...?

"I am not a liberator, the people liberate themselves...

(Che Guevara).

Theory of Everything No. 1

All that can be ever knowing
Of spirit, essence and energy
Is in the resonance of being.
Discover the All of Everything!
Mankind is given Creation's birthright:
To breathe unconditionally the love-light.
A notion – as above
        so below
Is found only in our heart of heart's
Voice of silence:
For you are never alone.
Go within, listen!
Un-common sense formed
Of all that is your own.
Dream into the undertone,
Or go without the experience
Of what you may be shown.

Theory of Everything No. 2

    Like is attractive to like, what's focused on or given away will return. If desire does not reappear it was not yours to keep, only give. Thus are prayers answered. In the releasing we learn how to live without baggage and stuff. This is the letting go and is loving; knowing how little or how much is actually enough; in freeing yourself you get to let go and love some more. What more do you need than this? No possessions except friendships and in those finding only love and freedom.

Spirituality.

A friend reading the manuscript before publication commented "it's not very Spiritual is it?"   Well, depends on what you mean by that word and no, this book is not wearing it's spirituality on it's sleeve, (sorry, bad pun again) ; it's more subtle than that.

Spiritual is the stuff of life that just gets on with it, knowing it'll all come out right in the end.   Funny how things work out mostly by themselves, by allowing, as discussed in the chapter on Relationships; the letting go of need for control.

State your wishes and intentions out loud and as the New Testament says somewhere; "whatsoever ye shall ask in prayer, believing, ye shall receive".*

Then there's the unsung heroes; millions of people uncomplainingly doing what needs to be done; always a help in any situation. What motivates them is not important or their personal convictions (if any), it stems from love, obviously... they're 'earth angels', most of 'em wouldn't recognize themselves as such, if you said anything about it.

Spirituality is not evangelical, it just is. All thoughts words and deeds that add positively to the mix is spirituality in action; it's your relationship to your personal God... or what else can you think it might be? Bless!

Matthew chapter 21, verse 22.

A Complementary Healing Practice.

There's about 250-odd recognized complementary healing practices (CHP) world wide, though few can name more than a dozen; they all have their place and no treatment is necessarily superior to any other; although it is true to say that one practice may work for you while another may not be as beneficial; as we are all different in size, shape, age, condition and so on.

"The most divine art is that of healing and if the art is divine it must occupy itself with the soul as well as the body; for no creature can be sound so long as the higher part of it is suffering".

(Pythagoras)

From this you'll note healing has been around for a very long time. So what is meant by 'healing'?   It's the transference of subtle light energies through the practitioner to the recipient, is holistic, which means the patient receives healing on all levels: mental, physical, spiritual and emotional as appropriate for them.

Healers are channellers of this energy from Source, (however you perceive this to be); a sacred and gentle art not to be taken lightly, though there's no need to be 'holy-moly' either.

There's a misnomer in using the term 'healer'; no-one 'heals' anybody.

Practitioners help the patient's own healing process. That's right!, humans can and do heal themselves as does most of nature, but often we need help so we go to a doctor, chemist, CHP, or other for medicine or other treatment.

I think of myself as a spiritual healer, others call themselves 'natural', 'hands-on', 'energy', ' bio-energy', or 'lightworker'. It's all the same. The term chosen is really only what the healer feels most comfortable with.

Spiritual healing is helped through relaxing the body, calming the mind as much as possible, releasing tensions and strengthening the immune system.

Treatment is gentle and non-invasive; the intent is to bring the patient to well-being and balance. The many complementary approaches to this end are equally viable, it's a question of which the patient feels happy with.

Contact healing is what it's called when the recipient is present, as healing can be given from a distance; generally known as 'absent healing', as it's not always necessary to actually touch the patient.

What's this about subtle light?   Quantum shows ultimately the whole Cosmos is made of light energy vibrations.   Subtle energy can't be measured; like the wind, can't see it but can feel the effect. (Don't blame me, Albert Einstein kicked this into being with his relativity theories, and came up with this name).

My personal experience of this is through patient's comments and thanks after a treatment; though I am aware of this energy flow too.

Here we are in the 21st century and folk are looking at more than one approach regarding their well-ness, for whatever personal reasons and taking responsibility for themselves, seeking to deal better with the stresses and strains of modern days' 'ever increasing pace of things world'.

This is bringing more open mindedness to viewing what's out there; from crystal therapy (say) which can trace it's history over millennia; to other relatively recent concepts.   New ideas coming along all the time.

An 'whole-istic' approach to self empowerment and healing is gaining greater acceptance by the allopathic medical community it is well to note.

Doctors are healers too, dedicating themselves to the relief of suffering by the methods they know and understand.   The more one learns about healing, the more is realized how much is still to be learnt; as no two treatments are ever the same, which is why healing is never routine; is always fresh and a beautiful thing to give someone.

All professions have standards and codes of conduct so that the public may know what's expected of practitioners and of the services provided.

To this end the British Alliance of Healing Associations' Code of Conduct provides guidelines and standards providing a framework of legal protection for both the individual member and the associate organizations; in keeping with the spirit of various relevant laws and Acts of Parliament.

Check your healer practitioner has an in-date membership card to his/her own Association, which will show they have been accredited or assessed and are covered by insurance for public liability and malpractice. Healing is a specialist function, a complementary therapy which doctors may delegate to, or a patient may request, on the N.H.S.

A number of CHP have, from time to time, been investigated by scientists wishing to 'prove' or otherwise, the effectiveness of these practices; but they all fail to come to any sensible conclusion, because they are testing a metaphysical property (subtle light) by physical means! Of course they'll get nothing from their instruments! ... I agree that some things are biologically implausible, but the fact remains that if you doubt the existence of a higher source of spirit and can only believe what you can measure with your ruler or see in your microscope... well you're limited, aren't you? And there are no limits, as has been discussed elsewhere in this book. In any event ask a patient about their treatment, and that's all you really need.

By all means seek out the fraudsters and charlatans, and with my blessing, but don't, Mr. Scientist tar us all with the same brush.

"Healing", papa would tell me, "is not a science, but the intuitive art of wooing nature".

(W.H.Auden)

A Healers Prayer.
(Anonymous).

Dearest God, to Thee I pray,
Heal my loved ones ill today,
Make them whole and healthy too,
And swift to recognize it's You
Who works the miracles of healing
In themselves, Thy grace revealing.
May their gratitude find vent
In thanking - not this instrument –
But Thee, from whom all blessings flow
To us Thy creatures here below.
I am but a channel lowly
For Thy healing, pure and holy.
Cleanse me, keep me true and bright,
Worthy to convey Thy light
To those who live in constant pain
And help Thee make them strong again.
Let me freely learn to serve
Those in need without reserve,

May I also from them learn
The patience I do not discern
In those who relish robust health
And do not understand the wealth
Of knowledge learnt, when all else fails
Only Thy grace and love prevails.

The Healer #1

Devices gauge no measure –
Nor can they!
Yet what we do is questioned,
By those who are unwilling to see how
This brilliant sacred breath…
Unconditionally flows.
Healing gifts dear patient are true…
And as one who well knows … it's enough…
For both me and you.

The Healer #2

Because I can
If it helps you,
That's all is to it.
Gifted from the Source,
A gentle force
Of spirit.
I am a 'sourcerer'
Who'll freely share
With any who ask
Of my healing and care.
All right,
Pray, go in peace...
And pain will release
To the light.

I Weep For The Generations.

I weep for the generations now
And for all those to follow,
Wondering if there'll be
Anything left tomorrow.
Anyone to tell if it ends in tears
And put out the fires in hell?
E'er since being here on wandering Earth
Mankind has been digging Her up
For all he's worth
In the unholy cause of financial gain;
Slowly destroying our beautiful home.
It's plain to see the strong preying on the weak;
The whales, forests, tribal lands and shores,
Bless all those who stand up,
Encourage them to speak!
There's enough for all, if we'll share
And care to take just enough, no more.
Still time to banish our shame

Of not having learned or being aware
There's only 'us' and no 'them'
Become the one's we've been waiting for!
Save the future and preserve Earth from ourselves.
I weep for all the generations, now
And for those who've yet to follow.
There'll be no need if we do take heed
Of the Tears of Sorrow.
The signs in the skies will be long time
Shining their story; brightly on all our tomorrows.

On Society.

In society the poor is always with us
Oft referred to by some, as scum;
Imprisoned by their lack, in having none.
The very rich is always with us
Oft referred to as cream and celebrity;
Imprisoned by wealth and position
And fear of loss. Their name is vanity.
Too much money is of use
Only in the getting of power to abuse.
Surely cream dissolves or just sours,
While scum floats on all surfaces.
They that begs, are they not dregs…
Kept at the bottom of the heap,
While those with too much, keep
On lying in the top places?
All have worth of relative value
However you revue it.
Ale is either light or dark,

Depends on how you brew it.
The rich in the community ...
Floats on top and you knew it
...as scum.
What do that say of society
From wherever you may view it?

To the Unknown Lover.

I'd like, love, you to like, know 'n' love me as
I like, know 'n' love me;
A little, not too much.
I'd like, love me to like, know 'n' love you as
I like, know 'n' love me;
A little, not too much.
Enough to touch hearts
And keep them safe;
You know…
A little, not too much.
Like, know, love; the eternal triangle;
Like attracts like
To know attracts knowing
Love attracts loving;
A little not too much.
Like = Love divided by Knowing
Know = Love divided by liking
Love = Liking multiplied by Knowing.

Awaiting.

Establishment,
Churchianity,
Politicking
Us and Them,
All lacking in any sorrows
And not measuring any worth…
While condemning the masses
Huddled, around their tv sets
Awaiting their jam tomorrows
In heaven,
Not on earth –
Not just yet.

Our Homes

Our homes are where our hearts are
Borne from stars and the dreamtime;
Our futures are garnered from the now place,
While heaven and hell can never rhyme
Nor are found in observable space.
Heaven is sacred, an unseen Above,
hell is anywhere with an absence of love,
And our homes are where our hearts are.

Jottings from my Blotting Papers.

Never before has been such a smile
of momentary grace…
wherein heaven itself slowed her pace
… tarried awhile.
I glance, in time to see
that smile
and all for me!

           X

look me up in my book,
look you up in your book
you know, the great works
that we are…
still in the writing.
and look for all the joys
bringing an end to the fighting.

Evolution : All things will come to pass,
          : today I live
          : kicking death in the ass.
          : and forgive me
Tomorrow : as I get to kick at death again…

— x —

You dream enough — you will survive
You want it enough — you will strive
to be better than ever before.
You good enough — you will make the score
that changes everything.

— x —

All that you dream is only true, even when seems it isn't;

all is working just fine for you, even when seems it doesn't.

Had a visit from the Angel in black,
said he wanted to take me back...
"like out of here, son"
Didn't he know only the good die young?
At that Black Angel was sorrowful
(for not being kept in the frame?)
my time is not now.
still playing my game,
don't call me, I'll call you...
And be late for my own funeral.

I spoke with my shoe cleaning angel
The other day – said was looking for
The angel in white who'd help me write
And show me about my p.c.
In her state of grace she told me, isn't one;
There's no computers in Heaven
They're all in that other place
Which comes as no surprise to me!

In the gallery the other day looking at paintings, heard a voice ask "what was the artist saying to us?" Holding in a laugh, holding back the tears unblinking, what's the artist saying?.. "I done this, what are *you* thinking?"

Musings

The greatest poem you've never read
Is the one unwritten, still on my head...

— x —

Heart
Like frozen pipes fit to burst,
She said yes!

— x —

stood in her shadow
ten feet tall —
in her eyes the future
that is All.

Sunny,
shadows entwine –
Togetherness.

                 – x –

Gained from tomorrow
To be lost in yesterday
The present moment.

                 – x –

LABELS ; " Either / Or"; Why not "As well"?

Brass plate
Hell's doorbell.
'Ring for a Tension'

— x —

Reality is only in the mind, not 'out there' for you to find,
A great place to visit... though be careful how long you stay...

— x —

Blessed are the Peacemakers
The ultimate 'movers and shakers'

— x —

Has it not already failed if you need apply 'fail – safe'?

Is it such a sin
Being alone in my head,
Wishing for a twin.

— x —

Grasses, fields and trees in nature are all green,
Relaxing and serene,
Slow, slow, slow.
Red is fire, heat, excitement, yeah
Go, go, go!
Conventional signs, such as traffic lights
Are out of sync. with nature
Surprise, surprise
But then, what do I know?

And Finally.

There has been a great deal already said about the end of the Mayan Long Calendar and what it means; a lot of it alarmist tosh.

The winter solstice in December 2012 marks the beginning of the end of the Age of Pisces and duality; heralding the beginning of the new Age of Aquarius, with the realization that we are all One.   A paradigm shift of consciousness; no more us and them; only us.

This will likely take centuries to become reality, so while we journey, as though to a friend's house; enjoy the ride, for it's never long...

Some reading that may help you further on your way –

Quantum Theory Cannot Hurt You.
Marcus Chow.
Marcus looked for this book, couldn't find, so wrote it himself, in good layman's language.

The Tao of Physics.
Fritjof Capra
A Classic, science meets Eastern philosophies.

Secrets In the Fields.
Freddy Silva
A most beautiful book about crop circles and a lot more…

The Secret History of The World.
Jonathan Black
A differing perspective.

'The Book of Secrets' / 'Power, Freedom, Grace'
Deepak Chopra

... or pretty much anything by this author

Crazy Wisdom ....
........Wes 'Scoop' Nisker

A romp through philosophies East and West.

Jonathan Livingstone Seagull / Illusions / The Messiah's Handbook
all by Richard Bach

Good books to start with; if you've read before, read 'em again!

The Alchemist.
Paulo Coehlo

...and pretty much any of his other books too.

THOTH, Architect of the Universe.
R. Ellis

A re-assessment of the design and function of great henges and pyramids and sacred geometry.

The Tao Te Ching.
Lao Tse

Several translations from ancient Chinese, which is why they vary. How Things Work, not much has changed in over 2600 years!

Attack of the Unsinkable Rubber Ducks.
Christopher Brookmeyer

How to spot phony psychics and is really entertaining fiction.

Wave Theory of Angels.

         Allison Macleod

A story of parallels centuries apart; good place to start on the quantum trail.

Two books about healing practice to start with —

Energy Medicine.

         Donna Eden

Your Healing Power.

         Jack Angelo

These next listed are absolute classics, their titles say it all —

The Power of Now

         Eckhart Tolle

The Prophet

         Kahil Gibran

Supernature

         Lyall Watson

Conversations With God 1

         Neale Donald Walsh

Spiritual Liberation

         Michael Bernard Beckwith

Secret Life of Plants

         Peter Tompkins and Chris Bird

This should be required reading in schools.

You Can Heal Your Life.

Louise L Hay

The book that got me out of a hole, re-kickstarting my present journey.

O.K. so where can I find these and any other book I may find interesting?

Have a look at Cygnus Books, they do discount mail order... and I have no business interests in them at all...

Cygnus, P.O.Box 15, LLANDEILO, South Wales, SA19 6YX   www.cygnus-books.co.uk

End Page.

Wisdom is not given, I've offered ideas, not wisdom; neither is truth taught...You got to live that.

And, everything in this book is true; unless it's not.

Acknowledgements.

Thank you dear Reader for allowing me to write this and to be published; for without you, where would authors be?   Thanks also to all who have helped in some way, with your inspiration, unwittingly or no, much valued.

About the Author

Richard Green is now retired, having been involved in grocery retail and wholesalers, after which was self employed with family in a pickles business (which was much more fun). Then as a come-in-handyman doing all manner of odd jobs, Now having a different kind of fun...He is a co-organizer of the world famous in Cornwall, Healing Light Festivals; and can be contacted via the 'about us' button at:

www.thehealinglightfestival.com